I

Museums

The Old and Not So Old

Muriel Bolger

ashfield
PRESS

Published in 2008 by
ASHFIELD PRESS • DUBLIN • IRELAND

Ashfield Press gratefully acknowledges all persons from the 31 museums in this publication, who generously supplied photographs and without whose help, this publication would not have been possible.

ISBN: 978-1-901658-69-9

A catalogue record for this book is available from the British Library.

This book is typeset by Ashfield Press
in 10 on 12 point Apple Garamond and Zapfino
Designed by SUSAN WAINE
Printed in Ireland by BETAPRINT LIMITED, DUBLIN

List of Museums

1. Bram Stoker Experience
2. Chester Beatty Library
3. Dublin City Hall – The Story of the Capital
4. Dublin Fire Brigade Museum
5. Dublinia
6. Dublin Writers Museum
7. Freemasons' Hall
8. Fry Model Railway Museum
9. GAA Museum
10. Garda Museum
11. Geological Museum
12. Guinness Storehouse
13. Imaginosity
14. Irish Jewish Museum
15. Irish Museum of Modern Art
16. James Joyce Tower
17. Kilmainham Gaol
18. Lambert Puppet Museum
19. National Maritime Museum
20. National Museum of Ireland – Archaeology
21. National Museum of Ireland – Decorative Arts & History
22. National Museum of Ireland – Natural History
23. National Print Museum
24. National Transport Museum
25. National Wax Museum
26. 35 North Great George's Street
27. Number 29 – Georgian Museum
28. Shaw Birthplace
29. The Pearse Museum
30. Tara's Palace Doll's House
31. Ye Olde Hurdy Gurdy Museum of Vintage Radios

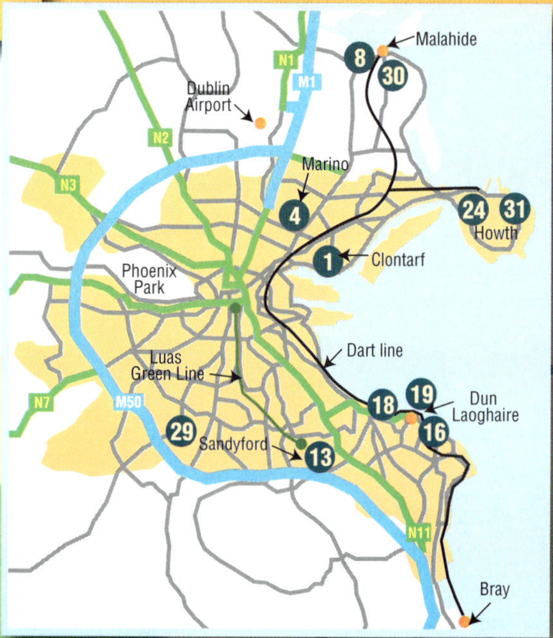
Malahide
8
30
N1
M1
Dublin Airport
N2
Marino
N3
4
24
31
Howth
1
Clontarf
Phoenix Park
Dart line
Luas Green Line
19
18
Dun Laoghaire
N7
M50
16
29
Sandyford
13
N11
Bray

Phoenix Park
21
25
Heuston Station
26
Guinness Brewery
15
Royal Hospital
12
17

Location of Museums

Introduction

Welcome to what I hope will prove to be a user-friendly guide to the museums of Dublin. Museums are for everyone and if you have not been given to visiting them in the past, associating them with boring school tours or such like, I promise that if you flick through these pages you'll find something to catch your eye, awaken curiosity and prompt a visit.

Whether you are interested in fossils or fashion, vampires or vehicles, writers or wirelesses, puppets or print, model railways or dolls houses, history, culture, art, the Orient, GAA, policing, Victorian life or James Joyce – there's bound to be something here for you.

The number of the capital's museums fluctuates and while researching and writing this collection the *Dublin Civic Museum* and the *Heraldic Museum* simply disappeared, with no plans for future relocation. The *National History Museum* building suffered a serious structural fault and will be closed for a few years for major renovation, while the really interesting *National Maritime Museum* in Dun Laoghaire is still undergoing its revamp and *The National Waxworks Museum* is on the move. A few others had no information

on whether or when they might reopen, among them *The Irish Labour History Museum*. *St. Enda's* in Rathfarnham, the school that was run by patriot Patraic Pearse will be back in business by the end of 2008.

However, despite these obstacles to writing a comprehensive guide, there were still thirty-one others to make it worthwhile! I've done my bit – taken the hard work out of it for you – now it's up to you to do your own exploration.

Enjoy.
Muriel Bolger

THE BRAM STOKER EXPERIENCE
Bar Code,
West Wood Health Club,
Clontarf,
Dublin 3
Tel 01 805 7824
www.thebramstokerdraculaexperience.com

Opening times: Fridays, 4-10pm; Saturdays, 12-10pm; Sundays, 12-10pm.

€ There is an entrance fee

Be prepared to be scared! The Bram Stoker Dracula Experience is really different, most interesting, and brilliantly entertaining. It's also pretty scary.

Although Bram Stoker wrote other things, it is for his blood curdling creation about an aristocratic vampire, *Count Dracula of Transylvania*, that most people remember his name. The sequel, *Dracula's Guest,* did not happen for some 17 years, two years after the author's death.

Stoker was born just a stone's throw from the museum opened to his memory in Clontarf, and his work continues to enjoy worldwide success, never having been out of print since it was published in 1897.

The first movie based on Dracula, *Nosferatu*, caused great controversy. It was released in Germany in 1922 with different character names and without permission. Stoker had married Florence Balcombe, a girl from the same crescent where they both lived – Oscar Wilde, another never out of print Dublin

writer, had previously courted her. As executor of her husband's estate, she knew that no permission had been given for the adaptations or film to be made of his work. A protracted court case saw her eventually receiving retribution and copies of all the prints of the film, which she had destroyed. Of course some survived and since then this tale of horror is credited with having inspired over 1,000 films worldwide.

The literary side of the museum gives you facts and figures about the author along with detailed information about why the book *Dracula* is considered as a pioneer in horror literature.

In the cultural part, amid flowing blood, bats, cobwebs, creepy things, coffins and chains, and of course, the infamous Torture Chamber, you can have your own encounter with the gothic world of the vampire!

2 Chester Beatty Librar

CHESTER BEATTY LIBRARY
Clock Tower Building,
Dublin Castle,
Dublin 2.
01 407 0750
www.cbl.ie

There is no entrance fee

Opening times:
October to April/Tuesdays to Fridays, 10-5pm; May to September/Mondays to Fridays, 10-5pm;
Saturdays, 11-5pm all year; Sundays 1-5pm all year.
Closed 1 January; Good Friday; 24, 25 and 26 December; and Monday public holidays.

Feted as European Museum of the Year in 2002, the Chester Beatty Library was also named Irish Museum of the Year in 2000. What makes this place so special, you may well ask? Well, its collections, of course, which are quite unique in Ireland.

A New Yorker, Sir Chester Beatty was born in 1875. He became a highly successful mining engineer,

who was often referred to as King of Copper for his success in Cripple Creek, Colorado where he made his millions. He moved to Dublin in the 1950s, was knighted in 1954 and became an honorary citizen of Ireland in 1957. Honoured with a state funeral when he died in1968, he gifted his treasures to the State.

Chester Beatty began amassing his considerable collection of manuscripts, drawings, rare books, miniature paintings, prints and

decorative arts from an early age. This collection captures a wonderful tapestry of creative expression from about 2700 BC to the present day.

Whilst the Library hosts other exhibitions too, its core collections are its main attraction. It showcases the diversity of the rich artistic treasures of the great religions and cultures. These span the globe from North Africa and Asia, to the Middle East and Europe. In this treasury you can enjoy the richness of Egyptian

papyrus texts, intricately illuminated copies of the Qur'an (Koran) and the Bible, and European medieval and renaissance manuscripts, among others.

The exhibits include clay tablets from Babylon dating from 2700 BC, Japanese woodblock prints, Chinese jade books and dragon robes, and Turkish and Persian paintings. The second floor, dedicated to the major religions, has custody of 250 manuscripts of the Koran from across the Muslim world, as well as one of the earliest Gospels. Life-size Buddha's from Burma and rhino cups from China are among the other curios on show.

This library and museum only moved from the suburbs to its present location in the historic Clock Tower Building of Dublin Castle in 2000. The glazed concourse area acts as a link between the restored 19th-century Clock Tower Building and the environmentally controlled exhibition spaces. There's a roof garden there, too.

3 Dublin City Hall

DUBLIN CITY HALL – THE STORY OF THE CAPITAL
Dublin City Hall,
Lord Edward Street, Dublin 8
Tel 01 222 2204
www.dublincity.ie

€ There is an entrance fee

Opening times: Mondays to Saturdays, 10-5.15pm;
Sundays and Bank Holidays, 2-5pm.

Every city has a story and Dublin is no exception. The beautifully restored vaults of Dublin Castle are the home to an exciting multi media look at the capital. Tracing its origins from the arrival of the Vikings, who settled on the banks of the River Liffey, it follows its development and expansion outside the old city walls, through times of invasions and insurrections, and the lives of its nationalists and its patriots.

Dublin's fortunes waxed and waned with the centuries, seeing thriving industry, occupation, dire poverty, famine years, emigration and a rising. The Story of the Capital brings to life the

he Story of the Capital

different ages and stages that have all contributed to making it the vibrant, cosmopolitan city it is today.

Since 1852, City Hall has been the centre of the municipal government so as a venue it's the perfect place for this museum. Among its items of interest are some 102 royal charters and the sword and mace of the city. You can also see the original Dublin City Seal and the Lord Mayor's Chain here, along with medieval manuscripts, period costumes and some contemporary artwork. Newsreel clips, video and interactive screens also contribute to the enjoyment of this intriguing insight into the passage of time.

Tightly interlinked with our history, the funerals of many notable political figures started from here, too – Charles Stewart Parnell, Jeremiah O'Donovan Rossa, Michael Collins and Arthur Griffith among them.

The actual building where The Story of the

Capital is displayed has its own place in the story. It was built between 1769 and 1779 as the Royal Exchange by a wealthy businessman, Thomas Cooley, who had won a design competition in which he beat his contemporary James Gandon into second place. It cost the princely sum of £58,000 to complete. Its formal entrance, the Rotunda, with its impressive gilded dome, murals, sculptures and mosaic and marble floor, is also open to the public and should not be missed on your visit.

4 Dublin Fire Brigade

Dublin Fire Brigade Museum,
Malahide Road,
Marino,
Dublin 3.
Tel. 01 833 8313 – phone for an appointment.
www.dublinfirebrigade.com

There is no entrance fee

All the Dublin Fire Brigade members do their training in the O'Brien Institute on Malahide Road. They also have their museum there. It's small but maintained with pride and respect. It doesn't house great fire tenders, some of which are in the National Transport Museum (see pages 62-64), but rather those precursors of modern day equipment.

You'll be able to see cart-type fire fighting units, which were manoeuvred by hand and considered state of the art when they were rolled out to contain blazes. There are memorabilia, insignias, badges, uniforms and other pieces of equipment used throughout the past decades.

One of the oldest exhibits is

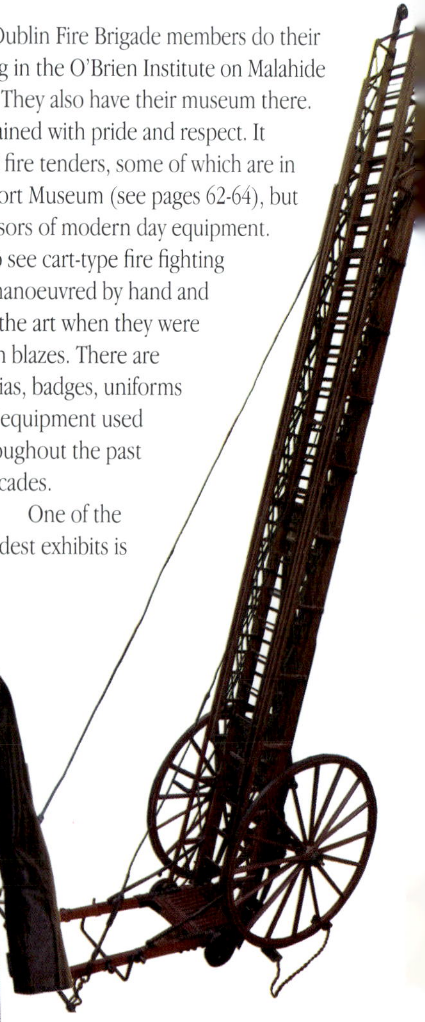

a wooden water pipe, dating from the 1600s. There are old search light holders and hoses, too, as well as lots of photographs, and proclamations from various Lord Mayors about having ladders and fire buckets at the ready for an emergency.

The museum is located in the former chapel of the O'Brien Institute, which was opened by Bridget O'Brien. It was financed by a trust set up in 1876, not for orphans but for children who had lost one parent. When she died, Bridget left the property to Dublin city, with a stipulation that it was to be used for training and educational purposes only and could not be sold. It is also protected as a listed building. The adjoining parade ground is used for fire and road accident training.

5 Dublinia

Dublinia is the Latin name for Dublin so by now you'll probably have guessed what this museum is all about. It uncovers its story from the formative period, charting the happenings from the arrival of the Anglo-Normans in 1170 to the closure of the monasteries in the 1540s.

This accurate depiction of life in medieval Dublin allows you witness the sights, sounds and even the smells of a bustling city, through life-sized reconstructions. You will find out how criminals were punished in the pillories; how heavy medieval armour really was, and how such inconveniences like a toothache were treated 700

DUBLINIA,
St. Michael's Hill, (Opposite Christ Church Cathedral)
Dublin 8.
Tel. 01 6794611
www.dublinia.ie

€ There is an entrance fee

Opening times: April to September/daily, 10-5pm;
October to March/Mondays to Fridays, 11-4pm;
Saturdays, Sundays and Bank Holidays, 10-4pm.
Closed 23, 24, 25 and 26 December and 17 March.

years ago! The highlights include a large-scale model of Dublin around 1500, with a busy medieval market, and the interior of a rich merchant's home.

Set right in the heart of old Dublin, many of the events portrayed actually happened in and around this locality. This interactive experience takes you from the capture of the city by Strongbow and his knights, up to the dramatic closure of the

DVBLINIA
& the Viking World

monasteries under Henry VIII in the 16th century. Strongbow is actually buried across the street in Christ Church Cathedral.

The Dublinia museum also houses a selection of artefacts from the National Museum of Ireland's excavations at Wood Quay close by. There's a well-preserved skeleton of a woman who lived in Dublin in the 12th century. After a little expert re-construction, you can now look this 900-year-old Dubliner in the eye.

The museum holds several Living History days throughout the year when visitors to Dublinia meet characters from the Viking and medieval periods as they walk through the exhibitions. These characters, in authentic costume, describe life as it was lived a thousand years ago. It almost makes you grateful for traffic jams! These days normally take place around Bank Holiday weekends and during the early summer.

6 Dublin Writers Mu

This capital city has produced countless famous writers and they are celebrated in the specially dedicated Dublin Writers Museum. It's a very accessible venue and a must for anyone wanting to discover more about the city's mammoth literary heritage and those who put it on the map. The Writers Museum is used as a writers centre, too, and the two museum rooms present a history of Irish literature from its beginnings up to recent times.

DUBLIN WRITERS MUSEUM

8 Parnell Square North,
Dublin 1.
Tel. 01 872 2077
www.writersmuseum.com

€ There is an entrance fee

Opening times: January to December/Mondays to Saturdays, 10-5pm; Sundays and public holidays, 11-5pm; late opening June, July and August/Mondays to Fridays, 10-6pm.

Here literary celebrities from the past three hundred years are brought to life through their books, letters, portraits and personal items. Located in an 18th century townhouse, there you'll find the first Gaelic translation of the Old Testament right up to modern classics. In the Gorham Library there's a large collection of first editions and various exhibits from the private lives of the writers, including correspondence and other memorabilia.

Among the pens, typewriters and smoking pipes there are some interesting personal possessions – Lady Gregory's lorgnette, Austin Clarke's desk, Samuel Beckett's telephone, Mary Lavin's teddy bear, Oliver St. John Gogarty's laurels and Brendan Behan's union card, complete with fingerprints.

You'll discover that if Samuel Beckett had not turned out to be one of the most influential writers of the 20th century, he may have made a name for himself on the cricket 1st XI at Trinity College, where Oscar Wilde showed great promise as a boxer!

You'll find an eclectic mix of Irish literature tomes from Swift's *Gulliver's Travels* and Stoker's *Dracula*, Wilde's *The Importance of Being Earnest* and Joyce's *Ulysses* to Beckett's *Waiting for Godot*. Most of these are first or early editions, recapturing the moment when they first surprised the world. There are books inscribed to Oliver St. John Gogarty by W.B. Yeats and to Brinsley MacNamara by James Joyce. There's also a first edition of Patrick Kavanagh's *The Great Hunger,* which includes a stanza in his own handwriting that the prudish publisher refused to print!

Among the portraits are some fine originals by artists such as Edward McGuire, Harry Kernoff, Patrick Swift and Micheal Farrell. Other memorabilia says a lot about the writers. There's a letter from Yeats to Frank O'Connor, a note from Sheridan to a creditor, a signed refusal from George Bernard Shaw to provide an autograph, a typically concise card from Samuel Beckett and a postcard from Brendan Behan from Los Angeles.

Upstairs the Gallery of Writers, with its portraits and busts, is used for receptions, exhibitions and special occasions. Room One takes the story through to the end of the 19th century and the beginning of the Literary Revival. Room 2 is entirely devoted to the great writers of the 20th century. Living writers, even those who have already established their place in history, are not included in the display. There's a Children's Room, too, *Seomra na nÓg,* which is devoted totally to children's literature.

Make sure you notice the grand staircase and wonderful Stapleton ceiling in this restored Georgian mansion on Parnell Square. The sumptuous plasterwork in the first floor Gallery of Writers is worth a visit alone.

Freemasons' Hall

7

For those with an interest in Freemasonry or with more than a mild curiosity of what those Masonic symbols and pageantry convey, a visit to the Freemasons' Hall will actually add to the mystique, rather than dispelling it.

This museum chronicles the history of Freemasonry, beginning with the formation of the Grand Lodge of Ireland in 1725. However it wasn't until the 1860s that the Order moved in to this competition-winning building on Molesworth Street, erected on what is believed to be the site of the townhouse of the first Grand Master, Richard, 1st Earl of Rosse.

FREEMASONS' HALL,
17 Molesworth Street,
Dublin 2.
Tel. 01 679 6799
www.irish-freemasons.org

Admission to the museum is free; tours of the building, €2 per head

Opening times: The museum is open all year round and from June to August scheduled guided tours of the building take place at 2.15pm. Outside these months, interested parties should telephone the curator first.

The exterior is an unusual mix of architectural styles incorporating Doric, Ionic and Corinthian influences. You can also see the Masonic square and compass on the pediment. Inside many of the original Victorian features still survive and there are several beautiful stained glass windows, some executed by the firm owned by the father of the renowned exponent of such art, Harry Clarke.

Included in the display items you'll be able to see some early and more modern magnificent Masonic jewels (medals to you and me!) sketches, items of 18th century regalia, pottery and glass, all decorated with the identifiable symbols of the all seeing eye and the mason's tools, which signify everything being aligned and righteous. There's also a life size reconstruction of a lodge meeting.

It's possible to visit the different rooms belonging to the various bodies within the organisation, and to see a portrait of the only female Mason in Ireland, Elizabeth St. Leger from Cork. She is reputed to have hidden in a grandfather clock but was discovered when it chimed, the muffled sound arousing suspicion. As she had overheard the secrets of the meeting it was felt that the one way to preserve their concealment was to induct her as a member.

There's a touch of Harry Potter magic about all of the ciphers and rooms in this building, where the various orders meet. These are all differently and ornately decorated. The Royal Arch Chapter room has an Egyptian theme. Be sure to check out the Prince Masons Chapter room and the Knights Templar Preceptory. This one is decorated like a medieval chapel, and its members dress like crusaders on ceremonial occasions. The Prince Masons Chapter room is a mixture of mock Tudor and Gothic and in the Grand Lodge room a huge black and white chequerboard carpet is said to have one extra white square – showing that good always overcomes evil.

Fry Model Railway 8

For little boys and those who never really grew up there is something magical about trains and train sets, so prepare to go back to playtime at the Fry Model Railway exhibition. Here a truly unique collection of handmade models of Irish trains, from the beginning of rail travel to modern times, will enchant. Believed to be one of the world's largest miniature systems, this working network covers an area of 2500 square feet (232.25 square metres), gauge '0' 1-43 scale.

This find is located in the old corn houses on the beautiful grounds of Malahide Castle and comprises numerous finely engineered models that were assembled as a result of a passionate interest in things to do with rolling stock. Its instigator was a railway engineer and draughtsman, Cyril Fry, who built this vast model, complete with lots of miniature vehicles, including buses, trams and lorries. It was to become a labour of love that lasted from the 1930s to the 1960s. The layout grew so big that it engulfed his bungalow in Churchtown and was later relocated to Malahide Castle.

There are miniatures of stations, streets and local landmarks, such as the River Liffey and Howth Head. Not only Ireland's largest miniature railway, the exhibition is unique in that it is a fully working railway system and continues to delight boys of all ages.

FRY MODEL RAILWAY
Malahide Castle Demesne,
Malahide, County Dublin.
Tel. 01 846 3779
fryrailway@dublintourism.ie

€ There is an entrance fee

Opening times: April to September/Mondays to Saturdays, 10-5pm; closed on Fridays; Sundays and public holidays, 2-6pm. Closed for lunch 1-2pm.

9 GAA Museum

For those who may not know, Ireland has its own national games, the most popular being Gaelic Football and Hurling. These are promoted by the Gaelic Athletic Association (GAA) or *Cumann Lúthchleas Gael* in the Irish language, which has some 800,000 members. This was founded in 1884.

Both are games of speed and skill. Gaelic football combines the dexterity of soccer, basketball and volleyball, resulting in a high-scoring game, not dissimilar to Australian Rules football. In fact there are matches between teams from both these disciplines in Ireland every year when they play to 'compromise' rules. Hurling is a fast and furious stick-and-ball game that combines many of the skills of field hockey, lacrosse and baseball, although it actually pre-dates all three. It is played with a hurley stick (*camán*) and a ball (*sliotar*).

The GAA Museum came about in response to a demand for somewhere to commemorate, recognise and celebrate the

GAA MUSEUM

Croke Park,
St Joseph's Avenue,
Croke Park, Dublin 3.
Tel. 01 8192323
www.museum.gaa.ie

€

There is an admission charge to the museum only, with an additional fee for the stadium tour. Group rates available

Opening times: The G.A.A. Museum is open throughout the year/Mondays to Saturdays, 9.30-5pm; Sundays, *12-5pm; in July and August, the museum is open Mondays to Saturdays, 9.30- 6pm.

*Except on match days when the museum opens at the same time as the turnstiles. On match days the museum is accessible to Cusack Stand ticket holders only and regular museum admission rates apply. The museum remains open until one hour after the end of the main match.

enormous contribution GAA has made not only to Irish sporting life, but also to its social and cultural life. It opened in 1998 and accommodates a vast collection of GAA memorabilia, including programmes, publications, letters, medals, hurleys and trophies. It's located beneath the stands in Croke Park Stadium in Dublin.

This stadium has played its own part in Irish history and has been the venue for many all Ireland battles and inter-county games. Visitors can enjoy a tour of the venue as well as having an in-depth look at one of the most historic and modern sporting arenas in the world. It has been used for over 100 years and the museum's friendly and knowledgeable guides will take you through the fascinating story, which is so much more than a question of sport to the nation. You'll get to see the dressing rooms, as well as the VIP section, the media centre and, of course, go pitch side.

The stadium has also been the venue of many high profile concerts including those of Celine Dion, Bon Jovi, Garth Brooks, Bruce Springsteen and Westlife. It was also the nerve centre of the Special Olympics World Summer Games in 2003. Another little bit of history was made in 2006 when the 'foreign' game of rugby was played on these sacred grounds. The Six Nations matches have been played here while their own rugby stadium was being revamped.

You'll find the museum under the Cusack Stand, named after Michael Cusack from County Clare, who founded the GAA. The tour lasts about one hour.

10 Garda Museum

Not just for budding sleuths and would be crime busters, the Garda Museum and Archives are located in a building that was a prison until the 1700s. Housed in the Record Tower in Dublin Castle, this historically interesting building dates back to 1205. The Record Tower was variously known as the Black Tower, the Gunner's Tower and the Wardrobe Tower, when it housed royal robes.

After 100 years this museum has acquired the safe from which the Irish crown jewels were stolen from Dublin Castle in 1907. This had been in custodial care in Kevin Street Garda Station and was released to the museum at the end of 2007.

GARDA MUSEUM
Record Tower, Dublin Castle,
Lord Edward Street, Dublin 2.
Tel. 01 666 9998
www.garda.ie

There is no entrance fee

Opening times: Visitors are welcome Mondays to Fridays, between 9-5pm. It is also possible to arrange a weekend visit by prior appointment.

Visitors will find material covering the history of the *Garda Síochána na h-Éireann* and facts concerning policing in Ireland prior to 1922. (Garda Síochána translates from Irish to Guardians of the Peace of Ireland.)

A uniformed and centralised police force was proposed for Ireland as early as the mid-18th century and in 1786, 33 years earlier than in London, the Dublin Metropolitan Police came into existence. This was to be followed in England in 1814 when Robert Peel, who later became a Conservative Prime Minister in England twice, pushed an act through Parliament to allow the appointment of paid magistrates.

The Museum is a popular venue with visitors and not only for those with policing connections. It contains photographs, archives and documents outlining the history and development of policing in the 19th and 20th centuries. There are uniforms, medals and artefacts relating to the establishment of the Irish Constabulary, later the Royal Irish Constabulary (R.I.C.), and the founding of the Dublin Police in 1836.

The Museum library holds a number of very interesting police related publications and is a great source for those doing research.

11 The Geological Museu

Geology is a science that deals with the history of the earth as recorded in rocks and that is exactly what you'll find at this museum. If you want to see a dinosaur's egg, dinosaur bones and meteorites then this is the place to go. You'll find the Geological Museum on the top floor of the Department of Geology in Trinity College, Dublin.

There you will discover the exhibition *The Story of the Earth,* with displays covering the complete range of geological topics. It's suitable for everyone, from the general public to students and school parties.

With over 80,000 specimens and collections that date from 1777, the mineral collection largely comes from the 1820s and is made up of both Irish and foreign specimens, while the main palaeontological holdings include Irish Silurian and Carboniferous invertebrates, Mesozoic ostracods and Upper Palaeozoic miospores.

Apart from the exhibits, take stock of the magnificent building where the Geology Department abides. Designed by Thomas Deane and Benjamin Woodward, it was inspired by the Byzantine architecture of Venice and dates back to 1853-57. Many of the interior and exterior carvings were completed by the Cork-born brothers, John and James O'Shea, and the exterior walls feature Wicklow granite and Portland Stone. The pillars, balustrades and banisters have examples of Irish marbles and Cornish serpentine, while the domed roof is made of blue, red and yellow enamelled bricks.

This building is the perfect place for such a museum as it takes you from seeing geology as nature intended to seeing it as man contrived it.

THE GEOLOGICAL MUSEUM
Department of Geology,
Trinity College,
Dublin 2.
Tel. 01 896 1477
www.tcd.ie

Opening times: Mondays to Fridays, 10-5pm.

There is no entrance fee

12 *Guinness Storehouse*

The name Guinness is synonymous with Dublin. It's the name of a drink made from water, barley, malt, hops and brewer's yeast. In 1759, Arthur Guinness started brewing ales at the St. James's Gate Brewery. He signed a 9,000-year lease at £45 per annum for the unused brewery. Now ten million glasses of Guinness are produced around the world every day.

This venue is hugely popular and was constructed in 1904 in the style of the Chicago school of architecture to house the Guinness fermentation process, which was carried out here until 1988. In November 2000, it opened its doors as a museum.

The core of the Storehouse building represents a giant pint glass, stretching from reception on the ground floor up to the Gravity Bar in the sky. If filled, this giant pint would hold approximately 14.3 million pints of Guinness.

Join the virtual master brewer to be guided through the brewing process, the tasting laboratory, transport exhibit, the workings of the craft of the cooper (Guinness used to make their own wooden barrels) and hear the tales about Guinness abroad.

Through the decades Guinness has had some unforgettable billboard and television ads and these may evoke memories as you enjoy them

GUINNESS STOREHOUSE
St. James's Gate,
Dublin 8.
Tel. 01 408 4800
www.guinness-storehouse.ie

€
There is an entrance fee

Opening times: All year Mondays to Sundays, 9.30-5pm; Late opening until 8pm in July and August. Closed Good Friday, Christmas Eve, Christmas Day and St. Stephen's Day.

on the second and fifth floors. One illustrator, John Gilroy, was responsible for many of the iconic ones from the 1930s to 1960s. There is a special exhibition of his original sketches, artwork and posters, drawn from the archives. With an eye to responsible consumption of alcohol there is a Choice Zone, where you can interact and study your own drinking habits.

And there's more… the fifth floor is where to learn how to pour the perfect pint in the Source Bar. By the time you reach the seventh floor, or the head of the pint, you will be rewarded with spectacular uninterrupted panoramas over the capital city and with a complimentary pint of the Black Stuff, of course.

13 Imaginosity Children

Based on the concept of 'Hands On, Minds On' learning, this is a place where creative learning and play connect. Hugely popular since it opened, this innovative space is located in the Plaza at Beacon South Quarter Square in Sandyford, Dublin. Imaginosity does not contain toys of yesteryear. Instead, it's a museum for children of 0-10 years and is richly packed with interactive experiences where they can roam freely, engaging in role-play activities and in doing things for themselves.

They can climb through a soaring tower, passing a tree house, through a ship, a wizard's lair, Rapunzel's castle and a

IMAGINOSITY
The Plaza,
Beacon South Quarter Square,
Sandyford,
Dublin 18.
Tel. 01 217 6130 – phone for bookings and opening times.
www.imaginosity.ie

€
There is an entrance fee

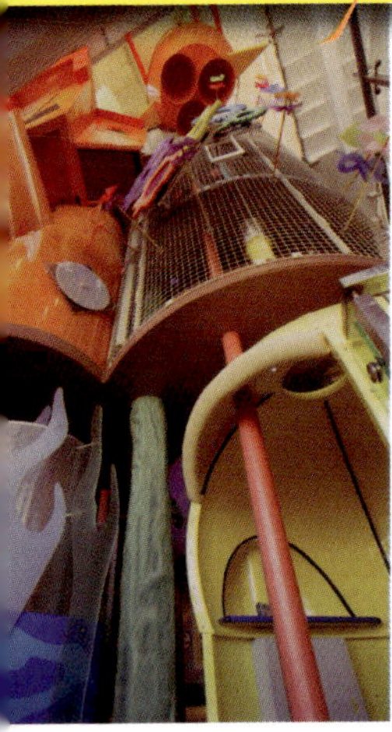

rocket as they do so. Elsewhere there is an adult world to be explored by learning how to build, hard hats and all; they can see what it's like to be a doctor or a banker or work in a television studio. In the surgery a drum beats in time with their heart and they can get a little practice in safe cracking.

In years to come, one wonders how many kids will say, 'I started my career in crime in Imaginosity', while others will say that it was planting vegetables in the Velcro garden that steered them on their career paths. Some future nutritionists may be in the making, too, as the little ones can work in a shop using old fashioned weighing scales and cash registers, learning about making good nutritional choices while they shop or operate the checkout and all without even realising it!

A central part of a visit here is learning about the building's 'green' features. By following a badger's paw prints right through to the lair on the roof, the little ones learn about the green technology behind the museum. It's a great way to introduce them to the principles of wind, solar energy and the concept of what a 'breathing' building is all about.

Groups and parties are welcome here and booking is required at certain times. It is easily accessible within walking distance of the Luas Stillorgan station.

14 Irish Jewish Museum

The Irish Jewish Museum is a real find. It's situated in the once highly Jewish populated area of Portobello, around South Circular Road, Dublin 8, which was known as Little Jerusalem. The museum is in the former Walworth Road Synagogue, which used to accommodate approximately 150/160 men and women and was made up of two adjoining terraced houses. Due to the movement of many of the Jewish community to the spreading suburbs of Dublin, as well as declining numbers, the Synagogue ceased to function as such in the mid-1970s.

It was almost ten years before it was to reopen with the establishment of the Irish Jewish Museum Committee. In fact it was opened by non other than the Irish-born former President of Israel, Dr. Chaim Herzog on 20 June 1985, during his State visit to Ireland. The museum, though small, preserves an important part of Ireland's cultural and historic heritage. There are some mementos of the Herzog family here, too.

The first Jewish settlers arrived in Ireland in 1660 and grew to quite a sizable population through the centuries. Although the material in the museum relates only to the last 150 years, it features a substantial collection of memorabilia relating to the communities that spread up around the country – in Belfast, Cork, Derry, Dublin, Limerick and Waterford.

THE IRISH JEWISH MUSEUM

3 Walworth Road,
Portobello,
Dublin 8.
Tel. 01 490 1857
www.isjm.org

There is no entrance fee

Opening times: May to September/Sundays, Tuesdays, Thursdays, 11-3.30pm; October to April /Sundays only, 10.30-2.30pm.

The first area is filled with photographs, paintings, testimonials and certificates, and focuses on the commercial and social life of the Jewish community. You'll be able to transport yourself back in time to the late 19th/early 20th century to see the inside of a typical Jewish family home in the neighbourhood, where the table is set for a Sabbath or festival meal.

Upstairs the original Synagogue, with all its ritual fittings, can be visited. There you'll also find that this main room still rings of spirituality and history, thanks in part to the largesse of Harold Smerling, an American businessman, who in the late 1980s, inspired by the museum, donated the money and resources to transform the former Ladies' Gallery into an extension of the exhibit. This space is now filled with artefacts donated by Holocaust survivors and items used on various Jewish holidays.

This little museum preserves an important part of Dublin and Jewish history and is really worth visiting.

15 Irish Museum of M

This museum has one of the best settings in the city, housed in the former Royal Hospital in Kilmainham with its enclosed courtyard and formal gardens. It's also right across from Kilmainham Gaol.

The 17th century Royal Hospital was founded in 1684 by James Butler, Duke of Ormonde and Viceroy to Charles II. It was a home for retired soldiers and remained as such for almost 250 years. It has a distinctly French feel to it and it's reputed to have been based on the architecture of *Les Invalides* in Paris. The buildings are arranged around a central courtyard with arched walkways surrounding this.

After major restoration the Royal Hospital Kilmainham opened as the Irish Museum of Modern Art in May 1991. It's now the country's leading national institution for the collection and presentation of modern and contemporary art, with in excess of 4,500 works. These have been acquired by purchase, donations and long-term loans, as

well as by the commissioning of new works. Apart from its impressive permanent collections the museum presents a wide variety of art in a dynamic programme of exhibitions.

The guiding principle behind this process is that the collection is firmly rooted in the present. The museum's acquisitions policy is to concentrate on the work of living artists, but it accepts donations and loans of more historical art objects with a particular emphasis on work from the 1940s onwards. Names you will find there include the Musgrave Kinley Outsider Art Collection and the Weltkunst Foundation Collection of British Art from the 1980s and '90s. The Madden Arnholz Collection of some 2,000 old master prints also forms a part of the IMMA Collection.

The permanent Collection of the IMMA comprises 1,650 works. These reflect some of the most exciting trends in Irish and international art with lens-based work by Gilbert and George, Marina Abramoviæ, Willie Doherty and Paul Seawright, installations by Ilya and Emilia Kabakov, Rebecca Horn and sculpture by Dorothy Cross, Kathy Prendergast, Juan Muñoz, Damien Hirst and Stephan Balkenhol, as well as paintings by Francesco Clemente, Tony O'Malley, Peter Doig and Peter Halley.

Some of the major donations include a wide variety of modern and contemporary art, including paintings, a large sculpture by Barry Flanagan and a film by Neil Jordan. Recent heritage gifts include *Dorothy* by Sean Scully and 50 works from the PJ Carroll & Co. Ltd. Art Collection.

IRISH MUSEUM OF MODERN ART
Royal Hospital,
Kilmainham, Dublin 8.
Tel. 01-612 9900
www.modernart.ie

There is no entrance fee

Opening hours: Tuesdays to Saturdays, 10-5.30pm; Wednesdays, 10.20-5.30pm; Sundays and Bank Holidays, 12-5.30pm. The museum is closed on Mondays.

16 James Joyce Tower

There are numerous Martello towers dotted along the east coast of Ireland. These were built in preparation for a possible invasion by Napoleon, which never happened. The tower at Sandycove was later to play a significant part in the life of one writer, James Joyce. It now holds a museum devoted to his life and works. Joyce used this tower as the setting for the opening chapter of his most famous work, *Ulysses*.

His stay here in the Joyce Tower, as it is known locally,

JAMES JOYCE TOWER
Forty Foot, Sandycove,
County Dublin.
Tel. 01 280 9265
www.dun-laoghaire.com

€ There is an entrance fee

Opening times: March to October/Mondays to Saturdays, 10-1, 2-5pm; Sundays and public holidays, 2-6pm.
Other months open by prior arrangement.

was brief, as in many of the other places he lived, but it was obviously an inspirational one with the sea spreading out below him. From the gun platform he could enjoy uninterrupted panoramas and the living room inside the tower is much as he described it in *Ulysses.*

The museum's collection includes letters, photographs, first and rare editions of his work, as well as personal possessions and items associated with the Dublin of *Ulysses*.

Ulysses was set on one day, 16th June 1904, a date now etched on Dubliners' minds as Bloomsday. It followed one Leopold Bloom as he went about his business and every year Joycean scholars and lovers of *Ulysses* gather to emulate Leopold's fictional footsteps. On that day, too, the James Joyce Tower museum opens from 8am-6pm for readings and a goodly bit of celebration.

17 Kilmainham Gaol

Kilmainham Gaol or Jail is much more than a prison. It witnessed bloodshed and executions. It housed traitors and patriots, political prisoners and zealots, murderers and brigands, and kept men, women and children incarcerated there.

Ireland's past has been turbulent and it was at the height of such turbulence that Kilmainham Jail was built in what was then the countryside outside Dublin. It was to witness many major events between the late 18th to early 20th century. These included the arrival of prisoners from the United Irish Rebellion of 1796, the Emmet Rebellion of 1803, the Great Famine of

KILMAINHAM JAIL
Inchicore Road, Kilmainham, Dublin 8.
Tel. 01 453 5984
www.kilmainham-gaol

€ There is an entrance fee

Opening times: April to September/ Mondays to Sundays, 9.30-6pm (last admission at 5pm); October to March/Mondays to Saturdays, 9.30-5.30pm (last admission at 4pm), Sundays,10-6pm (last admission at 5pm).

1845 to 1851, the Young Ireland Rebellion of 1848, the Fenian Rebellion of 1867, the Land War of the 1880s, the Easter Rising of 1916, the War of Independence and the Irish Civil War.

To put these dates in context… the jail opened in 1796, four years before the Act of Union that abolished the Irish Parliament in Dublin and made Ireland a part of the United Kingdom of Great Britain. It closed in 1924, two years after the signing of the Treaty that restored a measure of independence to the south of Ireland, a step that led ultimately to the declaration of a Republic in 1949.

Many of Ireland's most important historical figures spent time in the jail; some of them died there by firing squad, others by the hangman's noose. There are grim reminders dotted about and some spots are marked with small crosses. There's also a plaque marking the place where several of those involved in the 1916 Rising were executed.

Grace Gifford Plunkett, wife of Joseph Plunkett, painted a Madonna on one of the cell walls while she was held during the Civil War.

This jail is full of ghosts and in its own way probably encapsulates the fates and fortunes of Irish Republicanism better than anywhere else in the country.

18 Lambert Puppet Museu

If you grew up in Ireland, the characters of the Lambert Puppet Theatre will be no strangers to you. If you didn't, they will be sure to delight you just as they have done generations before you.

Eugene Lambert and his wife, Mai, established the company in 1972. Eugene always had an interest in puppetry and he had made a ventriloquist dummy called Frankie when he was young. Frankie later developed into Finnegan and he is still very much alive and performing today, a well-travelled gentleman having worked extensively in the UK and Ireland. He even went on to promote Ireland for the Irish Tourist Board, touring the USA, Japan and Australia.

However, the Lambert household grew and grew and with ten children to support on a refrigeration engineer's income, Eugene started to supplement his earnings by performing his Punch and Judy shows at parties and events. He and Mai attended an international puppet festival in Prague and decided that they would open a puppet theatre of their own. Since then it has become something of an institution, popular with both adults and

children alike. Finnegan's family also grew and a great favourite is the dog, Judge.

There are several shows performed at different times of the year and the puppet theatre is a great party venue because in addition to a performance the children get to visit the museum and go behind the scenes to meet some of their favourite puppets.

Several members of the Lambert family are now involved in this age-old tradition.

LAMBERT PUPPET MUSEUM
5 Clifden Lane,
Monkstown,
County Dublin.
Tel. 01 2800974 – phone for opening times.

www.lambertpuppettheatre.com

€

There is an entrance fee

19 National Maritime

Due to open again in 2009, the National Maritime Museum of Ireland is located in the former mariners' church in Haigh Terrace, Dun Laoghaire. The building itself is interesting. It was built in 1837 with a stipulation that one third of its 1,400 seats were to be set aside to accommodate the families of those in the seafaring, coastguard or revenue services. The church still functioned as such until 1971.

The seating has long been removed to make space for the museum exhibit but although the building has a new *raison d'être*, it still preserves its original character, features and records of its own unique history. Two prisoner's docks were located on either side of the stained glass windows of the west gallery so that those under punishment aboard ship could be kept under guard while still attending Sunday services!

This museum will have many new exhibits when it reopens after

NATIONAL MARITIME MUSEUM
Haigh Terrace, Dun Laoghaire,
County Dublin
www.dun-laoghaire.com

There is no entrance fee but donations are welcome

Opening times: This museum is closed until 2009.

extensive refurbishment but up to this among its treasures were the naval displays, which trace the history of the Irish service from before Independence to the present day. These include models, photos and documents, as well as uniforms connected with the Naval Force.

The Baily Optic, the light from the Baily Lighthouse across Dublin Bay in Howth, had shone there from 1902 until 1972, when the lighthouse was modernised. Originally gas, then oil powered, the light was equivalent to 2,000,000-candle power.

Another fascinating part of maritime history has to be the laying of trans-Atlantic cables on the bottom of the ocean. *The Great Eastern* was used for this and was the largest ship in the world when she was built in 1857. Its commander was a mariner supreme, Captain Halpin from Tinakilly House in County Wicklow. During her life, *The Great Eastern* was used first as a passenger ship, then a cable layer and finally as a showboat. She laid 2,600 miles of telegraphic cable in 1866, joining Europe to America. Among Captain Halpin's memorabilia and documents there's also a clockwork model of the ship that is over 100 years old.

The Bantry Boat was another popular curiosity, although it's now in The National Museum at Collins Barracks, during the renovations. This is a 38 feet long officers' barge that was captured during the failed French invasion of 1796. It was from the frigate *Resolue* and landed on Bere Island on 24 December that year. This boat is the only vessel to have survived from the invasion and despite being over 200 years old, is in excellent condition and still has the original blue, white and red paint of the new French Republic.

Although Ireland was neutral during World War II she rescued seamen from both sides of the conflict. One Irish merchant vessel, *Kerlogue*, was active at the time and on 29 December 1943 went to the rescue of the crews from two stricken German naval vessels in the Bay of Biscay, then a war zone. She rescued 168 crew from the sinking ships.

With its re-opening we can look forward to much more of the same exciting exhibits of things marine at this museum.

20 National Museum of

Fancy a walk back in time? Then the National Museum of Ireland – Archaeology on Kildare Street will transport you there. It's the place to go for a little time travelling – back to 7000 BC in fact, and along the way you may even come face to face with some of your ancestors in the form of some of the 'bog bodies' which were discovered, dating back to the Iron Age.

For sheer opulence you must visit the Treasury, where you can appreciate some outstanding examples of Celtic and medieval art. Here you'll find the famous Ardagh Chalice, the Tara Brooch and the Derrynaflan Hoard. You'll also be able to inspect the finest

Photographs coutesy of National Museum of Ireland

collection of prehistoric gold artefacts in Europe; these are in the *Ór* – Ireland's Gold exhibits.

Each age had its own mementos. There are artefacts from Viking Ireland, among them many finds which were unearthed just last century in the Wood Quay excavations in Dublin city centre. Medieval Ireland, 1150-1550, documents life in Ireland in the age of cathedrals, monasteries and castles.

The galleries are filled with relics and displays from the past, of things that shaped our history and which give us some indication of what life was like for our forefathers.

This building opened in 1890 and refurbishment on the exteriors is making sure it will look as good for the 21st century.

NATIONAL MUSEUM OF IRELAND – ARCHAEOLOGY
Kildare Street,
Dublin 2.
Tel. 01 677 7444
www.musem.ie

There is no entrance fee

Opening hours: Tuesdays to Saturdays, 10-5pm; Sundays, 2-5pm.
Closed Mondays.

21 National Museum of Irel

Photographs courtesy of National Museum of Ireland

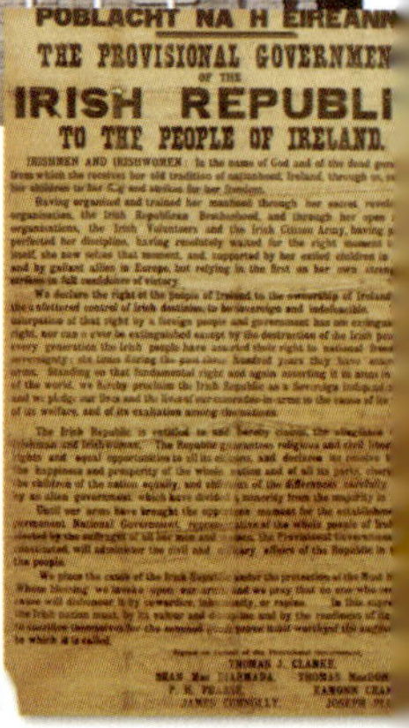
POBLACHT NA H EIREANN
THE PROVISIONAL GOVERNMEN
OF THE
IRISH REPUBLI
TO THE PEOPLE OF IRELAND.

Before you even go into the museum buildings at Collins Barracks you get a sense of history and excitement. Once inside you'll not be disappointed as this venue really does have something to appeal to everyone. Collins Barracks could be said to be the National Museum of Ireland's largest artefact, having had a unique history all of its own in another life. It was completely renovated and restored to become one of four venues belonging to the National Museum of Ireland, this being the museum of Decorative Arts & History, charting Ireland's economic, social, political and military progress through the ages.

Fashion lovers will relish the state of the art exhibitions on costume, clothing, and furniture. There are some iconic pieces by Eileen Gray, the Irish-born designer. The Irish silver collection is impressive, too. Amid the display cases and halls, the wide range of objects will keep you enthralled as you move from silver to objects of weaponry, ceramics and glassware, as well as examples of folk life and costume. The exhibitions have been designed in innovative and contemporary galleries.

Someone always wants to know what is the rarest exhibit. Well, it's the Fonthill Vase, a Chinese porcelain vase made about 1300 AD. This is widely renowned around the world as one of the best-documented pieces

of early porcelain. The William Smith O'Brien Gold Cup and the Eileen Gray chrome table are also among the highlights.

There's an *Out of Storage* section, which is housed in a double-height gallery, giving the visitor an impression of the range of artefacts in the reserve collections of the Museum of Decorative Arts and History, from large pieces of medieval wooden sculpture to delicate pieces of finely worked lace. The vast array of objects on display can be interpreted through interactive multimedia elements.

The *Irish Silver* collection is like a magnet and is one of the largest collections of Irish silver in the world. This traces the development of the silversmith's craft from the early 17th century to the present day. It addresses the evolution of design and examines the mining, assaying and crafting of this precious metal. It shows the various uses of silver – religious, domestic and ceremonial – and by means of vignettes seeks to place the objects in their historical and economic context.

Another very popular element is *The Way We Wore – 250 Years of Irish Clothing and Jewellery*. This displays clothing and jewellery worn in Ireland principally from the 1760s to the 1960s. Those who think solely of woollens and tweeds as Irish stereotypes can think again, as this exhibition shows that Ireland was up there in the style stakes of the fashion conscious of Europe.

NATIONAL MUSEUM OF IRELAND – DECORATIVE ARTS & HISTORY

Collins Barracks, Benburb Street,
Dublin 7.
Tel. 01 677 7444
www.musem.ie

There is no entrance fee

Opening hours: Tuesdays to Saturdays, 10-5pm; Sundays, 2-5pm. Closed Mondays.

22 National Museum of

This museum is closed for extensive renovation and modernisation following the collapse of a staircase in 2007. It will not reopen until 2010 but deserves to be included here as it was the oldest purpose-built museum in Ireland.

It opened in 1857 and is one of the very few Victorian cabinet style museums left in the world. It was home to a rich variety of animals, many of which are endangered or already extinct. When the Royal Dublin Society abandoned Leinster House, Leinster House became the seat of Irish Government or *the Dáil* in 1922. The original entrance to the Natural History Museum was through this building so it was given a new one directly onto Merrion Street.

The zoological exhibitions have been accumulated over two centuries and were drawn from a collection of over two million specimens. Much of this collection is a legacy of 19th century British colonialism. Included are samples of wildlife not only from Ireland, but also from around the world.

Children who visit are always impressed by the skeletons of the Giant Red Deer and by the numerous tiny insects hidden under their protective covers. There is a wonderful collection of animals, birds, insects and the celebrated Blaschka glass model collection. These were the work of Leopold (1822-1895) and Rudolf (1857-1939) Blaschka, a father and son partnership originally from Bohemia, who made amazingly accurate glass representations of flowers and marine life.

Other favourites included the armadillo and zebra, Spoticus the Giraffe and the mammoth 20metre-long whale skeleton that hung from the ceiling.

Happily these will all be re-instated when the museum is fully restored.

NATIONAL MUSEUM OF IRELAND
– Natural history
Merrion Street, Dublin 2.
Tel. 01 677 7444
www.musem.ie

There is no entrance fee

Opening times: This museum will be closed until 2010.

Photographs coutesy of National Museum of Ireland

23 National Print Museu

We all take printing for granted nowadays with printers on our desks and at our fingertips. Now we simply insert a sheet of paper, press the print command and hey presto, we can have our photos and documents printed in black and white or glorious colour.

But it wasn't always so. Formerly every single individual letter had to be picked from printers' trays and each word spelt backwards so that when dipped in ink and printed on the paper it would read correctly. Those who worked on such tasks were known as compositors.

Printing did not arrive in Ireland until 1551, when Humphrey Powell printed *The Boke of Common Praier.* This first book in Irish type was paid for by Queen Elizabeth I and was probably

NATIONAL PRINT MUSEUM
Garrison Chapel,
Beggars Bush,
Haddington Road,
Dublin 4.
Tel. 01 660 3770
www.iol.ie/~npmuseum

There is no entrance fee

Opening times: Mondays to Fridays, 9-5pm; Saturdays and Sundays, 2-5pm, all year around.

manufactured in London. In 1571, an unidentified printer printed *Aibidil Gaoidheilge agus Caiticiosma*, the first book using the Irish (Gaelic) characters. In 1618, the London Stationers' Company was granted the King's Printer's patent in Ireland and set up a printing house in Dublin. The King's Printer was confined to government printing and this led to a few other presses being

established in Dublin and the provinces in the mid-17th century. The first one outside Dublin was set up by Thomas Bourke in Waterford in 1643, followed by Kilkenny in 1646 and in Cork in 1649.

The story of the National Print Museum began in 1985, when new technology and computers were fast making old skills and large printing obsolete. Work commenced on saving machinery from what is probably best known in printing terms as the 'hot metal' era. A committee was formed representing all sections of the printing industry, including commercial printers, suppliers, newspapers, trade unions and academia, who combined their knowledge to preserve this vital part of our heritage. In 1991, the Office of Public Works donated the former Garrison Chapel in Beggars Bush Barracks, Dublin to become the National Print Museum. The building, which is under a preservation order, has its own unique history to tell, too.

Not only was this museum established to document the history of printing in Ireland but also to retain the skills relating to the craft of printing and to create a permanent working exhibition. It opened in 1996 and now has a vast collection of over 10,000 objects that cover the whole range of the craft in Ireland. This is made up of machinery and artefacts, including

printing blocks, metal and wooden moveable type, ephemera, photographs, books, pamphlets, periodicals and much more. The associated skills of bookbinding and stitching are also represented, as is a unique pen-ruling machine, used to line thousands of children's copybooks for many years past. Headline events in world history are commemorated in framed newspaper pages, which adorn the walls of the gallery upstairs.

There's a wonderfully comprehensive video presentation that enhances any visit here.

One exhibit that grabs a lot of attention is the bookbinders' banner from 1887. Painted by a Dublin artisan, this was carried by union members in a Labour Day demonstration in Dublin in 1894. This is unique in its design as it is double-sided and fully painted – and a much treasured part of the collection.

This is a fascinating place to visit and it will make you realise how far we have come since Gutenberg's first printed book in 1455 – and just how fantastic your desktop printer really is!

24 National Transport

Museum

A visit to this museum will evoke memories for many. Remember the green buses with the step at the back? The Howth tram? Bedford vans? Well, they're all there in glorious splendour in the Heritage Depot of Howth Castle Demesne, thanks to Captain Christopher Gainsford-St. Lawrence.

This collection is due to the sheer determination of a few enthusiasts who wouldn't take no for an answer. In 1949, the Transport Museum Society of Ireland began with an abortive effort to preserve three Dublin trams. Vandalism and the elements defeated many of the TMSI's pioneering preservation attempts, resulting in the loss of irreplaceable treasures. Totally voluntary, the Society became a limited company in 1971 and is now a registered charity, operating to international museum standards. Today, it has a remarkable collection, broken into five main categories – passenger, commercial, fire and emergency, military and utility.

Sixty out of the 100 vehicles currently in Howth are on display

and others can be inspected by prior arrangement. The oldest items date from 1883, the newest, 1984.

The collection is Ireland's only comprehensive assembly of public service and commercial road transport. Even the humblest vehicles are noteworthy. Many are the sole existing examples of once familiar types, several others are very rare and some are unique. Portraying the golden age of commercials, the collection includes some 30 marques. All four Irish commercial vehicle builders are represented.

The vehicles have come to the museum by donation, loan or purchase. Serious space limitations and the need to house every one have resulted in having to display them more closely than is desirable, but no one is complaining as they walk about inspecting them and remembering other times.

NATIONAL TRANSPORT MUSEUM
Heritage Depot,
Howth Demesne, Howth,
Dublin 13.
Tel. 01 832 0427
www.nationaltransportmuseum.org

€ There is an entrance fee

Opening times: September to May/Saturdays, Sundays & Bank Holidays, 2-5pm; June to August/Mondays to Saturdays, 10-5pm.

The Wax Museum is in transit but will probably be installed in its new premises in Smithfield by the time this guide reaches the bookshelves.

There is something about wax museums that always intrigues. The figures seem to be watching you wherever you go and you always have the feeling that one of them is going to come alive and give chase!

This museum gives an overall life-size view of Irish history and events, with wax figures of Irish people of historical, political, literary, theatrical and sporting fame. Although there will be new additions in the Smithfield exhibition space, some old favourites are perennially popular – the likes of rich, famous and megastars

NATIONAL WAX WORKS MUSEUM
Smithfield,
Dublin 1.
www.dublintourist.com

€

There will be an entrance fee

Opening hours: No more details are available at time of going to press, other than a 2008 opening is on the cards.

Bono, Elvis, Michael Jackson and Phil Lynott, will all feature.

Younger children love the *Children's World of Fairytale and Fantasy* and you can hear their delight as they recognize different characters in this entertaining adventure as they wander through the Fairytale Kingdom in search of the magical lamp and the genie!

The main section deals broadly with characters and issues in the development of Ireland and features wax figures of many famous and infamous political names. You'll find the 1916 Rebellion leaders, as well as Robert Emmet, Wolfe Tone and Charles Stewart Parnell, and you can tell former *Taoisigh* (Prime Ministers) and Presidents what you really think about them as you pass.

Of course our literary heritage has not been neglected here either and there are many famous writers and playwrights making their presence felt – Joyce and Yeats among them.

Who knows who'll have made it into the final cut with the new opening?

26 35 North Great George

James Joyce, one of Dublin's most celebrated writers, never actually lived in this typical Georgian house in North Great George's Street. He did however have a connection with it through Prof. Denis J. Maginni who ran a Dance Academy there. Maginni was a well-known and colourful character in Dublin and appears several times in James Joyce's *Ulysses*. In the 'Wandering Rocks' episode he is described as wearing a "silk hat, slate frockcoat with silk facings, white kerchief tie, tight lavender trousers, canary gloves and pointed patent boots". The Maginni Room, now the Café Ulysses, was originally the dining room of the house.

The James Joyce Centre is here, just 300 metres from the northern end of O'Connell Street, the city's main thoroughfare. The house, a typical period residence of its time, is in what was then one of Dublin's finest addresses. It was built in 1784 by Francis Ryan for Valentine Brown, the Earl of Kenmare, who used it as his townhouse. The ornate plasterwork was done by Michael Stapleton, one of the finest stuccodores of the time. By 1982, twelve houses on this street had been demolished by the City

35 NORTH GREAT GEORGE'S STREET
Dublin 1.
Tel. 01 878 8547
www.jamesjoyce.ie

€
There is an entrance fee

Opening time: Tuesdays to Saturdays, 10-5pm.

Council as dangerous buildings, including the house next door. Number 35 was saved by a Joycean scholar who also lives on the street. The Centre opened in June 1996 and is run by members of the Monaghan family, descendants of Joyce's sister, May.

The Joyce family lived in houses similar to this one, and in the Library there's a folder with a list of Joyce's Dublin addresses, complete with photographs and other details.

Two copies of portraits of Joyce hang in the Library, one by Jacques Emile Blanche, the other by Irish artist, Harry Kernoff. Some of the highlights of the permanent displays include furniture from the apartment of Paul Léon, Joyce's friend and advisor, and of course James Joyce's death mask. Out in the yard at the back there's the original hall door from No. 7 Eccles Street. In *Ulysses* this is Leopold Bloom's address, but the house itself was demolished to make way for an extension to the Mater Hospital.

In the Guinness Library there are many translations of Joyce's works, alongside volumes about him and his creations. Joyce had a great knack of word portraiture, of capturing the places, the people, the food, the atmosphere and the smells that were his Dublin. Through interactive installations and films, you may delve into the novel *Ulysses*, its historical backdrop and its publishing controversies, and learn more about Joyce's life.

27 *Number Twenty Nine*

For a little bit of social history this venue has got to be a favourite with Dubliners and visitors alike. In the heart of Georgian Dublin, Number Twenty Nine Fitzwilliam Street was one of ten houses on Fitzwilliam Street Lower and on Mount Street Upper restored by the Electricity Supply Board in 1988. It had previously and very controversially knocked down a whole row of similar ones to build modern offices.

This house tells the story of its first occupant, a Mrs. Olivia Beatty, who moved there in November 1794. She had married at 21, in St Anne's Church on Dawson Street, and she and her husband, Edward, had seven children. She was widowed at 33. In the late 1700s, their narrow back garden would have looked out

NUMBER TWENTY-NINE FITZWILLIAM STREET LOWER

29 Fitzwilliam Street Lower,
Dublin 2.
Tel. 01 702 6165
www.esb.ie/numbertwentynine

€
There is an entrance fee

Opening hours: Tuesdays to Saturdays, 10-5pm; Sundays, 1-5pm. The house is closed on Mondays, Good Friday and for two weeks at Christmas.

on the open countryside to the sea at Irishtown. Now it's central city! Life in this Georgian period is reflected throughout the house, revealing much of what it was like for middle class Dubliners back then in a real Upstairs, Downstairs fashion.

Among the most popular exhibits are two 19th century dolls houses in the nursery. The children's quarters were tucked away in the attic at the top of the house. These were sparsely decorated and had no carpets or decorative plasterwork, unlike the luxury to be found below. In these times, boys were educated and three of them, Edward, Frederick and Thomas, went to Trinity College. In contrast their sister Olivia married at just 15. She would probably have had a governess and only studied English, history and geography, as well as music, needlework, and probably a little French.

The furniture, glassware, ceramics and painting on display are mostly Irish, dating from the late 18th century or early 19th century. There were no flush toilets and water had to be carried up and down the stairs for ablutions.

The kitchen was the nerve centre of such Georgian houses and some impressive dining and entertaining would have taken place upstairs. After dinner the gentlemen remained at the table for some port and cigars, while the ladies 'retired'. In reality this gave the chaps a chance to use the chamber pots provided in the

dining room! The ladies attended to their business upstairs. The first floor or *piano nobile* was the most important public room and it was in here that the family treasures were displayed. Visitors are always amazed at how small the bedchambers are compared with the generous proportions of the reception rooms.

To meet the rising demand of an expanding and in some cases an affluent Dublin, manufacturers of luxury goods prospered in the city at this time. In 1798, Dublin boasted at least 25 coachbuilders, over 30 gold and silversmiths, and nearly 50 cabinetmakers. These were all supplying the residents of the large mansions found in Merrion Square and St. Stephen's Green and increasingly to those moving into the more modest developments in areas such as Mountjoy Square and Fitzwilliam Street Lower.

Although much of the fabric of the original house had not survived, great consideration went into the development of this exhibition and into putting the pieces of the historical jigsaw together accurately. Many original patterns were used in features such as the wallpapers, carpets, and curtains. Number Twenty Nine tells the previously untold story of middle class home life in a key period in the history of the capital.

Don't miss it!

Shaw Birthplace 28

George Bernard Shaw is one Ireland's foremost playwrights. He was born in this terraced house in Synge Street, in the then suburbs of Dublin, on 26 July 1856. Outside a plaque says, 'Author of Many Plays'. This simple accolade doesn't say he was one of Ireland's four winners of the Nobel Prize for Literature or that he also won an Oscar. In fact this modest dwelling gives no indication or clues to his future success. His Victorian home and early life mirror simplicity. The house was later restored to its Victorian charm where, as well as portraying what life was like for the Shaw family, it creates a nostalgia for the life, times and things which may have inspired this writer to create some of his memorable characters.

Shaw, who lived here until 1876, penned *Pygmalion,* (later made into the film *My Fair Lady*), *Man and Superman*, and *John Bull's Other Island* among his many works.

The house has been furnished in Victorian style, recreating the atmosphere of Shaw's early days. You can visit the kitchen, with its dearth of appliances and amenities, the maid's room, the nursery, the drawing room, the master bedroom and George Bernard's box room. In the cosy drawing room, where musical evenings played a big part in the lives of this family, the piano is open and the sheet music ready, just waiting to be played. There's a tiny back garden and it's here the little privy is located.

Shaw moved to London when he was 20 and married Charlotte Payne-Townshend, whom he survived. They made their home in Ayot St. Lawrence in Hertfordshire in a house now called Shaw's Corner. He died there, aged 94, from problems exacerbated by injuries incurred falling from a ladder.

SHAW BIRTHPLACE
33 Synge Street,
Dublin 8.
Tel. 01 475 0854
www.visitdublin.com

€
There is an entrance fee

Opening Times: May to September/Mondays, Tuesdays, Thursdays and Fridays, 10-1pm and 2-5pm; Saturdays, Sundays and public holidays, 2-5pm. Closed from October to April and every Wednesday.

The Pearse Museum 29

The Pearse Museum (*Músaem na bPiarsach*) is located in the grounds of the former experimental school started and run by the patriot, Patrick Pearse at Saint Enda's or Scoil Eanna. The Museum has been closed for extensive renovations but is due to reopen with a better than ever

THE PEARSE MUSEUM
St. Enda's Park,
Grange Road,
Rathfarnham
Tel 01 493 4208 Email: kilmainhamgaol@opw.ie I

There is no entrance fee

Opening Times: Pearse Museum: Closed temporarily
St. Enda's Park: Average Length of Visit: 1–2 hours
November to January: Daily 10-4.30pm, February to March: Daily 10-5.30pm, April and September: Daily 10-7.00pm, May to August: Daily 10-1pm and 2-5.30pm. Closed 24 - 26 December

exhibition shortly. Currently only the Nature Room and grounds are open to the public.

Patrick Pearse was a teacher, poet, writer, nationalist and leader of the 1916 Easter Rising. He was executed for the part he played in it on May 3rd, 1916.

Visitors going to St Enda's during the renovations will have to content themselves with a 20-minute audiovisual show entitled 'This Man Kept a School'. Once opened again the museum will house a collection photos and works that will offer a retrospective look at his life and the history of the times in which Pearse lived.

However many people come to St Enda's for the other main attractions, the Nature Study room, detailing Irish flora and fauna and the wonderful grounds. There is a well signposted trail, which takes you by its riverside walks, waterfall and walled garden, and although close to the city you feel you are way out in the countryside.

Groups are welcome and guided tours given, but these must be booked in.

Tara's Palace 30

Take a trip down memory lane at Tara's Palace, undoubtedly one of the world's most significant dolls houses. It was inspired by Sir Neville Wilkinson's celebrated Titania's Palace of 1908. Ron and Doreen McDonnell sought to recapture the magic when they began the creation of their own work of art, Tara's Palace, in 1980.

A lesser-known masterpiece, but a masterpiece no less, this is now housed in Malahide Castle, Dublin. The house itself is built in 1/12th scale and is influenced by three of Ireland's grandest houses - Castletown House, Leinster House and Carton House, all 18th century mansions of architectural merit.

Tara's Palace has 25 furnished rooms and was built to raise money for children's charities. It's meticulously constructed and took over a decade to complete. It has real mahogany furniture and china replicas. There are paintings by leading Irish artists and miniature furnishing pieces adorn the state rooms and private apartments.

The displays are augmented and peopled by a collection of dolls, while the nursery has its own collection of antique toys.

For the intricacy and accuracy of the reproductions and the delicacy and detail of the fine points of fashion and décor, this palace deserves more than a passing glance.

TARA'S PALACE
The Courtyard,
Malahide Castle Demesne,
Malahide, County Dublin.
Tel. 01 846 3779
www.malahidecastle.com

€

There is an entrance fee, which is donated to charity

Opening times: 8 April to 30 September/Mondays to Fridays, 10.45-4.45pm; Saturdays, Sundays and public holidays, 11.30-5.30pm. It is closed during the winter months.

31 Ye Olde Hurdy-Gurd

If you recall your grandfather talking about crystal sets then this place will jog some distant thoughts. Do you remember the crackly reception as you tried to listen to Friday Night is Music Night on the BBC and the way the sound always seemed to fade just at the announcements? Do you remember when the radio went off in the afternoons to commence broadcasting again in the evening? And those sponsored programmes at lunchtime? Well, if you do then you are definitely a child of the radio era and you'll love this museum!

Located in the Martello Tower it houses a fine collection of exhibits that chronicle the history of telecommunications from the

YE OLDE HURDY-GURDY MUSEUM OF VINTAGE RADIO
Martello Tower, Abbey Street,
Howth,
County Dublin.
Tel. 086 815 4189
www.qsl.net/ei5em/museum.html

€

There is an entrance fee

Opening Times: May to October, 11-5pm daily; November to April, 11-4pm, weekends only.

1840s to date. The setting is perfect as this tower has historic links with Marchese Guglielmo Marconi and Lee de Forest, two of the fathers of wireless, who conducted early experiments from it in the 1900s. It was also the site of an early cable station.

In the eclectic collections prepare to be mesmerized at the many early examples of Morse equipment, wind-up gramophones, crystal sets, valve radios and other pieces of equipment. The walls are lined with posters, old record sleeves and singles, and there's a wonderful air of nostalgia here.

For the curator, Pat Herbert, this is so obviously a labour of love and he's always happy to demonstrate some of the many working exhibits and share their provenance with you.